Theseus

Plutarch

translated by

John Dryden

Another Leaf Press

```
    *
   ***
  ******
   ***
    *


    *
   ***
  *******
 **********
  ******
   ***
    *


    *
   ***
  ******
   ***
    *
```

ANOTHER LEAF PRESS

2013

Theseus

As geographers, Sosius, crowd into the edges of their maps parts of the world which they do not know about, adding notes in the margin to the effect, that beyond this lies nothing but sandy deserts full of wild beasts, unapproachable bogs, Scythian ice, or a frozen sea, so, in this work of mine, in which I have compared the lives of the greatest men with one another, after passing through those periods which probable reasoning can reach to and real history find a footing in, I might very well say of those that are farther off, Beyond this there is nothing but prodigies and fictions, the only inhabitants are the poets and inventors of fables; there is no credit, or certainty any farther. Yet, after publishing an account of Lycurgus the lawgiver and Numa the king, I thought I might, not without reason, ascend as high as to Romulus, being brought by my history so near to his time. Considering therefore with myself

> *Whom shall I set so great a man to face?*
> *Or whom oppose? who's equal to the place?*

(as Aeschylus expresses it), I found none so fit as him that peopled the beautiful and far-famed city of Athens, to be set in opposition with the father of the invincible and renowned city of Rome. Let us hope that Fable may, in what shall follow, so submit to the purifying processes of Reason as to take the character of exact history. In any case, however, where it shall be found contumaciously slighting credibility, and refusing to be reduced to anything like probable fact, we shall beg that we may meet with candid readers, and such as will receive with indulgence the stories of antiquity.

Theseus seemed to me to resemble Romulus in many particulars. Both of them, born out of wedlock and of uncertain parentage, had the repute of being sprung from the gods.

Both warriors; that by all the world's allowed.

Both of them united with strength of body an equal vigor mind; and of the two most famous cities of the world the one built Rome, and the other made Athens be inhabited. Both stand charged with the rape of women; neither of them could avoid domestic misfortunes nor jealousy at home; but towards the close of their lives are both of them said to have incurred great odium with their countrymen, if, that is, we may take the stories least like poetry as our guide to the truth.

The lineage of Theseus, by his father's side, ascends as high as to Erechtheus and the first inhabitants of Attica. By his mother's side he was descended of Pelops. For Pelops was the most powerful of all the kings of Peloponnesus, not so much by the greatness of his riches as the multitude of his children, having married many daughters to chief men, and put many sons in places of command in the towns round about him. One of whom named Pittheus, grandfather to Theseus, was governor of the small city of the Troezenians, and had the repute of a man of the greatest knowledge and wisdom of his time; which then, it seems, consisted chiefly in grave maxims, such as the poet Hesiod got his great fame by, in his book of Works and Days. And, indeed, among these is one that they ascribe to Pittheus,--

> *Unto a friend suffice*
> *A stipulated price;*

which, also, Aristotle mentions. And Euripides, by calling Hippolytus "scholar of the holy Pittheus," shows the opinion that the world had of him.

Aegeus, being desirous of children, and consulting the oracle of Delphi, received the celebrated answer which forbade him the company of any woman before his return to Athens. But the oracle being so obscure as not to satisfy him that he was clearly forbid this, he went to Troezen, and communicated to Pittheus the voice of the god, which was in this manner,--

> *Loose not the wine-skin foot, thou chief of men,*
> *Until to Athens thou art come again.*

Pittheus, therefore, taking advantage from the obscurity of the oracle, prevailed upon him, it is uncertain whether by persuasion or deceit, to lie with his daughter Aethra. Aegeus afterwards, knowing her whom he had lain with to be Pittheus's daughter, and suspecting her to be with child by him, left a sword and a pair of shoes, hiding them under a great stone that had a hollow in it exactly fitting them; and went away making her only privy to it, and commanding her, if she brought forth a son who, when he came to man's estate, should be able to lift up the stone and take away what he had left there, she should send him away to him with those things with all secrecy, and with injunctions to him as much as possible to conceal his journey from every one; for he greatly feared the Pallantidae, who were continually mutinying against him, and despised him for his want of children, they themselves being fifty brothers, all sons of Pallas.

When Aethra was delivered of a son, some say that he was immediately named Theseus, from the tokens which his father had *put* under the stone; others that he received his name afterwards at Athens, when Aegeus *acknowledged* him for his son. He was brought up under his grandfather Pittheus, and had a tutor and attendant set over him named Connidas, to whom the Athenians, even to this time, the day before the feast that is dedicated to Theseus, sacrifice a ram, giving this honor to his memory upon much juster grounds than to Silanio and Parrhasius, for making pictures and statues of Theseus. There being then a custom for the Grecian youth, upon their first coming to man's estate, to go to Delphi and offer first-fruits of their hair to the god, Theseus also went thither, and a place there to this day is yet named Thesea, as it is said, from him. He clipped only the fore part of his head, as Homer says the Abantes did. And this sort of tonsure was from him named Theseis. The Abantes first used it, not in imitation of the Arabians, as some imagine, nor of the Mysians, but because they were a warlike people, and used to close fighting, and above all other nations accustomed to engage hand to hand; as Archilochus testifies in these verses: --

> *Slings shall not whirl, nor many arrows fly,*
> *When on the plain the battle joins; but swords,*
> *Man against man, the deadly conflict try,*
> *As is the practice of Euboea's lords*
> *Skilled with the spear.--*

Therefore that they might not give their enemies a hold by their hair, they cut it in this manner. They write also that this was the reason why Alexander gave command to his captains that all the beards of the Macedonians should be shaved, as being the readiest hold for an enemy.

Aethra for some time concealed the true parentage of Theseus, and a report was given out by Pittheus that he was begotten by Neptune; for the Troezenians pay Neptune the highest veneration. He is their tutelar god, to him they offer all their first-fruits, and in his honor stamp their money with a trident.

Theseus displaying not only great strength of body, but equal bravery, and a quickness alike and force of understanding, his mother Aethra, conducting him to the stone, and informing him who was his true father, commanded him to take from thence the tokens that Aegeus had left, and to sail to Athens. He without any difficulty set himself to the stone and lifted it up; but refused to take his journey by sea, though it was much the safer way, and though his mother and grandfather begged him to do so. For it was at that time very dangerous to go by land on the road to Athens, no part of it being free from robbers and murderers. That age produced a sort of men, in force of hand, and swiftness of foot, and strength of body, excelling the ordinary rate, and wholly incapable of fatigue; making use, however, of these gifts of nature to no good or profitable purpose for mankind, but rejoicing and priding themselves in insolence, and taking the benefit of their superior strength in the exercise of inhumanity and cruelty, and in seizing, forcing, and committing all manner of outrages upon every thing that fell into their hands; all respect for others, all justice, they thought, all equity and humanity, though naturally lauded by common people, either out of want of courage to commit injuries or fear to receive them, yet no way concerned those who were strong enough to win for themselves. Some of these, Hercules destroyed and cut off in his passage through these countries, but some, escaping his notice while he was passing by, fled and hid themselves, or else were spared by him in contempt of their abject submission; and after that Hercules fell into misfortune, and, having slain Iphitus, retired to Lydia, and for a long time was there slave to Omphale, a punishment which he had imposed upon himself for the murder, then, indeed, Lydia enjoyed high peace and security, but in Greece and the countries about it the like villanies again revived and broke out, there being none to repress or chastise them. It was therefore a very hazardous journey to travel by land from Athens to Peloponnesus; and Pittheus, giving him an exact account of each of these robbers and villains, their strength, and the cruelty they used to all strangers, tried to persuade Theseus to go by sea. But he, it seems, had long since been secretly fired by the glory of Hercules, held him in the highest estimation, and was never more satisfied than in listening to any that gave an account of him; especially those that had seen him, or had been present at any action or saying of his. So that he was altogether in the same state of feeling as, in after ages, Themistocles was, when he said that he could not sleep for the trophy of Miltiades; entertaining such admiration for the virtue of Hercules, that in the night his dreams were all of that hero's actions. And in the day a continual emulation stirred him up to perform the like. Besides, they were related, being born of cousins-german. For Aethra was daughter of Pittheus, and Alcmena of Lysidice; and Lysidice and Pittheus were brother and sister, children of Hippodamia and Pelops. He thought it therefore a dishonorable thing, and not to be endured, that Hercules should go out everywhere, and purge both land and sea from wicked men, and he himself should fly from the like adventures that actually came in his way; disgracing his reputed father by a mean flight by sea, and not showing his true one as good evidence of the greatness of his birth by noble and worthy actions, as by the tokens that he brought with him, the shoes and the sword.

With this mind and these thoughts, he set forward with a design to do injury to nobody, but to repel and revenge himself of all those that should offer any. And first of all, in a set combat, he slew Periphetes, in the neighborhood of Epidaurus, who used a club for his arms, and from thence had the name of Corynetes, or the club-bearer; who seized upon him, and forbade him to go forward in his journey. Being pleased with the club, he took it, and made it his weapon, continuing to use it as Hercules did the lion's skin, on whose shoulders that served to prove how huge a beast he had killed; and to the same end Theseus carried about him this club; overcome indeed by him, but now, in his hands, invincible.

Passing on further towards the Isthmus of Peloponnesus, he slew Sinnis, often surnamed the Bender of Pines, after the same manner in which he himself had destroyed many others before. And this he did without having either practiced or ever learnt the art of bending these trees, to show that natural strength is above all art. This Sinnis had a daughter of remarkable beauty and stature, called Perigune, who, when her father was killed, fled, and was sought after everywhere by Theseus; and coming into a place overgrown with brushwood shrubs, and asparagus-thorn, there, in a childlike, innocent manner, prayed and begged them, as if they understood her, to give her shelter, with vows that if she escaped she would never cut them down nor burn them. But Theseus calling upon her, and giving her his promise that he would use her with respect, and offer her no injury, she came forth, and in due time bore him a son, named Melanippus; but afterwards was married to Deioneus, the son of Eurytus, the Œchalian, Theseus himself giving her to him. Ioxus, the son of this Melanippus who was born to Theseus, accompanied Ornytus in the colony that he carried with him into Caria, whence it is a family usage amongst the people called Ioxids, both male and female, never to burn either shrubs or asparagus-thorn, but to respect and honor them.

The Crommyonian Sow, which they called Phaea, was a savage and formidable wild beast, by no means an enemy to be despised. Theseus killed her, going out of his way on purpose to meet and engage her, so that he might not seem to perform all his great exploits out of mere necessity; being also of opinion that it was the part of a brave man to chastise villainous and wicked men when attacked by them, but to seek out and overcome the more noble wild beasts. Others relate that Phaea was a woman, a robber full of cruelty and lust, that lived in Crommyon, and had the name of Sow given her from the foulness of her life and manners, and afterwards was killed by Theseus. He slew also Sciron, upon the borders of Megara, casting him down from the rocks, being, as most report, a notorious robber of all passengers, and, as others add, accustomed, out of insolence and wantonness, to stretch forth his feet to strangers, commanding them to wash them, and then while they did it, with a kick to send them down the rock into the sea. The writers of Megara, however, in contradiction to the received report, and, as Simonides expresses it, "fighting with all antiquity," contend that Sciron was neither a robber nor doer of violence, but a punisher of all such, and the relative and friend of good and just men; for Aeacus, they say, was ever esteemed a man of the greatest sanctity of all the Greeks; and Cychreus, the Salaminian, was honored at Athens with divine worship; and the virtues of Peleus and Telemon were not unknown to any one. Now Sciron was son-in-law to Cychreus, father-in-law to Aeacus, and grandfather to Peleus and Telamon, who were both of them sons of Endeis, the daughter of Sciron and Chariclo; it was not probable, therefore, that the best of men should make these alliances with one who was worst, giving and receiving mutually what was of greatest value and most dear to them. Theseus, by their account, did not slay Sciron in his first journey to Athens, but afterwards, when he took Eleusis, a city of the Megarians, having circumvented Diocles, the governor. Such are the contradictions in this story. In Eleusis he killed Cercyon, the Arcadian, in a wrestling match. And going on a little farther, in Erineus, he slew Damastes, otherwise called Procrustes, forcing his body to the size of his own bed, as he himself was used to do with all strangers; this he did in imitation of Hercules, who always returned upon his assailants the same sort of violence that they offered to him; sacrificed Busiris, killed Antaeus in wrestling, and Cycnus in single combat, and Termerus by breaking his skull in pieces (whence, they say, comes the proverb of "a Termerian mischief"), for it seems Termerus killed passengers that he met, by running with his head against them. And so also Theseus proceeded in the punishment of evil men, who underwent the same violence from him which they had inflicted upon others, justly suffering after the manner of their own injustice.

As he went forward on his journey, and was come as far as the river Cephisus, some of the race of the Phytalidæ met him and saluted him, and, upon his desire to use the purifications, then in custom, they performed them with all the usual ceremonies, and, having offered propitiatory sacrifices to the gods, invited him and entertained him at their house, a kindness which, in all his journey hitherto, he had not met.

On the eighth day of Cronius, now called Hecatombaeon, he arrived at Athens, where he found the public affairs full of all confusion, and divided into parties and factions, Aegeus also, and his whole private family, laboring under the same distemper; for Medea, having fled from Corinth, and promised Aegeus to make him, by her art, capable of having children, was living with him. She first was aware of Theseus, whom as yet Aegeus did not know, and he being in years, full of jealousies and suspicions, and fearing every thing by reason of the faction that was then in the city, she easily persuaded him to kill him by poison at a banquet, to which he was to be invited as a stranger. He, coming to the entertainment, thought it not fit to discover himself at once, but, willing to give his father the occasion of first finding him out, the meat being on the table, he drew his sword as if he designed to cut with it; Aegeus, at once recognizing the token, threw down the cup of poison, and, questioning his son, embraced him, and, having gathered together all his citizens, owned him publicly before them, who, on their part, received him gladly for the fame of his greatness and bravery; and it is said, that when the cup fell, the poison was spilt there where now is the enclosed space in the Delphinium; for in that place stood Aegeus's house, and the figure of Mercury on the east side of the temple is called the Mercury of Aegeus's gate.

The sons of Pallas, who before were quiet, upon expectation of recovering the kingdom after Aegeus's death, who was without issue, as soon as Theseus appeared and was acknowledged the successor, highly resenting that Aegeus first, an adopted son only of Pandion, and not at all related to the family of Erechtheus, should be holding the kingdom, and that after him, Theseus, a visitor and stranger, should be destined to succeed to it, broke out into open war. And, dividing themselves into two companies, one part of them marched openly from Sphettus, with their father, against the city, the other, hiding themselves in the village of Gargettus, lay in ambush, with a design to set upon the enemy on both sides. They had with them a crier of the township of Agnus, named Leos, who discovered to Theseus all the designs of the Pallantidae. He immediately fell upon those that lay in ambuscade, and cut them all off; upon tidings of which Pallas and his company fled and were dispersed.

From hence they say is derived the custom among the people of the township of Pallene to have no marriages or any alliance with the people of Agnus, nor to suffer the criers to pronounce in their proclamations the words used in all other parts of the country, *Acouĕtĕ Leoi* (Hear ye people), hating the very sound of Leo, because of the treason of Leos.

Theseus, longing to be in action, and desirous also to make himself popular, left Athens to fight with the bull of Marathon, which did no small mischief to the inhabitants of Tetrapolis. And having overcome it, he brought it alive in triumph through the city, and afterwards sacrificed it to the Delphinian Apollo. The story of Hecale, also, of her receiving and entertaining Theseus in this expedition, seems to be not altogether void of truth; for the townships round about, meeting upon a certain day, used to offer a sacrifice, which they called Hecalesia, to Jupiter Hecaleius, and to pay honor to Hecale, whom, by a diminutive name, they called Hecalene, because she, while entertaining Theseus, who was quite a youth, addressed him, as old people do, with similar endearing diminutives; and having made a vow to Jupiter for him as he was going to the fight, that, if he returned in safety, she would offer sacrifices in thanks of it, and dying before he came back, she had these honors given her by way of return for her hospitality, by the command of Theseus, as Philochorus tells us.

Not long after arrived the third time from Crete the collectors of the tribute which the Athenians paid them upon the following occasion. Androgeus having been treacherously murdered in the confines of Attica, not only Minos, his father, put the Athenians to extreme distress by a perpetual war, but the gods also laid waste their country; both famine and pestilence lay heavy upon them, and even their rivers were dried up. Being told by the oracle that, if they appeased and reconciled Minos, the anger of the gods would cease and they should enjoy rest from the miseries they labored under, they sent heralds, and with much supplication were at last reconciled, entering into an agreement to send to Crete every nine years a tribute of seven young men and as many virgins, as most writers agree in stating; and the most poetical story adds, that the Minotaur destroyed them, or that, wandering in the labyrinth, and finding no possible means of getting out, they miserably ended their lives there; and that this Minotaur was (as Euripides hath it)

> *A mingled form, where two strange shapes combined,*
> *And different natures, bull and man, were joined.*

But Philochorus says that the Cretans will by no means allow the truth of this, but say that the labyrinth was only an ordinary prison, having no other bad quality but that it secured the prisoners from escaping, and that Minos, having instituted games in honor of Androgeus, gave, as a reward to the victors, these youths, who in the mean time were kept in the labyrinth; and that the first that overcame in those games was one of the greatest power and command among them, named Taurus, a man of no merciful or gentle disposition, who treated the Athenians that were made his prize in a proud and cruel manner. Also Aristotle himself, in the account that he gives of the form of government of the Bottiaeans, is manifestly of opinion that the youths were not slain by Minos, but spent the remainder of their days in slavery in Crete; that the Cretans, in former times, to acquit themselves of an ancient vow which they had made, were used to send an offering of the first-fruits of their men to Delphi, and that some descendants of these Athenian slaves were mingled with them and sent amongst them, and, unable to get their living there, removed from thence, first into Italy, and settled about Japygia; from thence again, that they removed to Thrace, and were named Bottiaeans and that this is the reason why, in a certain sacrifice, the Bottiaean girls sing a hymn beginning *Let us go to Athens*. This may show us how dangerous a thing it is to incur the hostility of a city that is mistress of eloquence and song. For Minos was always ill spoken of, and represented ever as a very wicked man, in the Athenian theaters; neither did Hesiod avail him by calling him "the most royal Minos," nor Homer, who styles him "Jupiter's familiar friend;" the tragedians got the better, and from the vantage ground of the stage showered down obloquy upon him, as a man of cruelty and violence; whereas, in fact, he appears to have been a king and a lawgiver, and Rhadamanthus a judge under him, administering the statutes that he ordained.

Now when the time of the third tribute was come, and the fathers who had any young men for their sons were to proceed by lot to the choice of those that were to be sent, there arose fresh discontents and accusations against Aegeus among the people, who were full of grief and indignation that he, who was the cause of all their miseries, was the only person exempt from the punishment; adopting and settling his kingdom upon a bastard and foreign son, he took no thought, they said, of their destitution and loss, not of bastards, but lawful children. These things sensibly affected Theseus, who, thinking it but just not to disregard, but rather partake of, the sufferings of his fellow citizens, offered himself for one without any lot. All else were struck with admiration for the nobleness and with love for the goodness of the act; and Aegeus, after prayers and entreaties, finding him inflexible and not to be persuaded, proceeded to the choosing of the rest by lot. Hellanicus, however, tells us that the Athenians did not send the young men and virgins by lot, but that Minos himself used to come and make his own choice, and pitched upon Theseus before all others; according to the conditions agreed upon between them, namely, that the Athenians should furnish them with a ship, and that the young men that were to sail with him should carry no weapon of war; but that if the Minotaur was destroyed, the tribute should cease.

On the two former occasions of the payment of the tribute, entertaining no hopes of safety or return, they sent out the ship with a black sail, as to unavoidable destruction; but now, Theseus encouraging his father and speaking greatly of himself, as confident that he should kill the Minotaur, he gave the pilot another sail, which was white, commanding him, as he returned, if Theseus were safe, to make use of that; but if not, to sail with the black one, and to hang out that sign of his misfortune. Simonides says that the sail which Aegeus delivered to the pilot was not white, but

> *Scarlet, in the juicy bloom*
> *Of the living oak-tree steeped,*

and that this was to be the sign of their escape. Phereclus, son of Amarsyas, according to Simonides, was pilot of the ship. But Philochorus says Theseus had sent him by w:Scirus, from Salamis, Nausithoüs to be his steersman, and Phaeax his look-out-man in the prow, the Athenians having as yet not applied themselves to navigation; and that Scirus did this because one of the young men, Menesthes, was his daughter's son; and this the chapels of Nausithoüs and Phaeax, built by Theseus near the temple of Scirus, confirm. He adds, also, that the feast named Cybernesia was in honor of them. The lot being cast, and Theseus having received out of the Prytaneum those upon whom it fell, he went to the Delphinium, and made an offering for them to Apollo of his suppliant's badge, which was a bough of a consecrated olive tree, with white wool tied about it.

Having thus performed his devotion, he went to sea, the sixth day of Munychion, on which day even to this time the Athenians send their virgins to the same temple to make supplication to the gods. It is farther reported that he was commanded by the oracle at Delphi to make Venus his guide, and to invoke her as the companion and conductress of his voyage, and that, as he was sacrificing a she goat to her by the seaside, it was suddenly changed into a he, and for this cause that goddess had the name of Epitrapia.

When he arrived at Crete, as most of the ancient historians as well as poets tell us, having a clue of thread given him by Ariadne, who had fallen in love with him, and being instructed by her how to use it so as to conduct him through the windings of the labyrinth, he escaped out of it and slew the Minotaur, and sailed back, taking along with him Ariadne and the young Athenian captives. Pherecydes adds that he bored holes in the bottoms of the Cretan ships to hinder their pursuit. w:Demon writes that Taurus, the chief captain of Minos, was slain by Theseus at the mouth of the port, in a naval combat, as he was sailing out for Athens. But Philochorus gives us the story thus: That at the setting forth of the yearly games by king Minos, Taurus was expected to carry away the prize, as he had done before; and was much grudged the honor. His character and manners made his power hateful, and he was accused moreover of too near familiarity with Pasiphae, for which reason, when Theseus desired the combat, Minos readily complied. And as it was a custom in Crete that the women also should be admitted to the sight of these games, Ariadne, being present, was struck with admiration of the manly beauty of Theseus, and the vigor and address which he showed in the combat, overcoming all that encountered with him. Minos, too, being extremely pleased with him, especially because he had overthrown and disgraced Taurus, voluntarily gave up the young captives to Theseus, and remitted the tribute to the Athenians. w:Clidemus gives an account peculiar to himself, very ambitiously, and beginning a great way back: That it was a decree consented to by all Greece, that no vessel from any place, containing above five persons, should be permitted to sail, Jason only excepted, who was made captain of the great ship Argo, to sail about and scour the sea of pirates. But Daedalus having escaped from Crete, and flying by sea to Athens, Minos, contrary to this decree, pursued him with his ships of war, was forced by a storm upon Sicily, and there ended his life. After his decease, Deucalion, his son, desiring a quarrel with the Athenians, sent to them, demanding that they should deliver up Daedalus to him, threatening, upon their refusal, to put to death all the young Athenians whom his father had received as hostages from the city. To this angry message Theseus returned a very gentle answer, excusing himself that he could not deliver up Daedalus, who was nearly related to him, being his cousin-german, his mother being Merope, the daughter of Erechtheus. In the meanwhile he secretly prepared a navy, part of it at home near the village of the Thymœtadæ, a place of no resort, and far from any common roads, the other part by his grandfather Pittheus's means at Troezen, that so his design might be carried on with the greatest secrecy. As soon as ever his fleet was in readiness, he set sail, having with him Daedalus and other exiles from Crete for his guides; and none of the Cretans having any knowledge of his coming, but imagining, when they saw his fleet, that they were friends and vessels of their own, he soon made himself master of the port, and, immediately making a descent, reached Gnossus before any notice of his coming, and, in a battle before the gates of the labyrinth, put Deucalion and all his guards to the sword. The government by this means falling to Ariadne, he made a league with her, and received the captives of her, and ratified a perpetual friendship between the Athenians and the Cretans, whom he engaged under an oath never again to commence any war with Athens.

There are yet many other traditions about these things, and as many concerning Ariadne, all inconsistent with each other. Some relate that she hung herself, being deserted by Theseus. Others that she was carried away by his sailors to the isle of Naxos, and married to Œnarus, priest of Bacchus; and that Theseus left her because he fell in love with another,

> *For Ægle's love was burning in his breast;*

a verse which Hereas, the Megarian, says, was formerly in the poet Hesiod's works, but put out by Pisistratus, in like manner as he added in Homer's Raising of the Dead, to gratify the Athenians, the line

> *Theseus, Pirithoüs, mighty sons of gods.*

Others say Ariadne had sons also by Theseus, Œnopion and w:Staphylus; and among these is the poet Ion of Chios, who writes of his own native city

> *Which once Œnopion, son of Theseus, built.*

But the more famous of the legendary stories everybody (as I may say) has in his mouth. In Paeon, however, the Amathusian, there is a story given, differing from the rest. For he writes that Theseus, being driven by a storm upon the isle of Cyprus, and having aboard with him Ariadne, big with child, and extremely discomposed with the rolling of the sea, set her on shore, and left her there alone, to return himself and help the ship, when, on a sudden, a violent wind carried him again out to sea. That the women of the island received Ariadne very kindly, and did all they could to console and alleviate her distress at being left behind. That they counterfeited kind letters, and delivered them to her, as sent from Theseus, and, when she fell in labor, were diligent in performing to her every needful service; but that she died before she could be delivered, and was honorably interred. That soon after Theseus returned, and was greatly afflicted for her loss, and at his departure left a sum of money among the people of the island, ordering them to do sacrifice to Ariadne; and caused two little images to be made and dedicated to her, one of silver and the other of brass. Moreover, that on the second day of Gorpiaeus, which is sacred to Ariadne, they have this ceremony among their sacrifices, to have a youth lie down and with his voice and gesture represent the pains of a woman in travail; and that the Amathusians call the grove in which they show her tomb, the grove of Venus Ariadne.

Differing yet from this account, some of the Naxians write that there were two Minoses and two Ariadnes, one of whom, they say, was married to Bacchus, in the isle of Naxos, and bore the children Staphylus and his brother; but that the other, of a later age, was carried off by Theseus, and, being afterwards deserted by him, retired to Naxos with her nurse Corcyna, whose grave they yet show. That this Ariadne also died there, and was worshiped by the island, but in a different manner from the former; for her day is celebrated with general joy and revelling, but all the sacrifices performed to the latter are attended with mourning and gloom.

Now Theseus, in his return from Crete, put in at Delos, and, having sacrificed to the god of the island, dedicated to the temple the image of Venus which Ariadne had given him, and danced with the young Athenians a dance that, in memory of him, they say is still preserved among the inhabitants of Delos, consisting in certain measured turnings and returnings, imitative of the windings and twistings of the labyrinth. And this dance, as Dicaearchus writes, is called among the Delians, the Crane. This he danced round the Ceratonian Altar, so called from its consisting of horns taken from the left side of the head. They say also that he instituted games in Delos where he was the first that began the custom of giving a palm to the victors.

When they were come near the coast of Attica, so great was the joy for the happy success of their voyage, that neither Theseus himself nor the pilot remembered to hang out the sail which should have been the token of their safety to Aegeus, who, in despair at the sight, threw himself headlong from a rock, and perished in the sea. But Theseus, being arrived at the port of Phalerum, paid there the sacrifices which he had vowed to the gods at his setting out to sea, and sent a herald to the city to carry the news of his safe return. At his entrance, the herald found the people for the most part full of grief for the loss of their king, others, as may well be believed, as full of joy for the tidings that he brought, and eager to welcome him and crown him with garlands for his good news, which he indeed accepted of, but hung them upon his herald's staff; and thus returning to the seaside before Theseus had finished his libation to the gods, he stayed apart for fear of disturbing the holy rites, but, as soon as the libation was ended, went up and related the king's death, upon the hearing of which, with great lamentations and a confused tumult of grief, they ran with all haste to the city. And from hence, they say, it comes that at this day, in the feast of Oschophoria, the herald is not crowned, but his staff, and all who are present at the libation cry out *eleleu, iou, iou,*, the first of which confused sounds is commonly used by men in haste, or at a triumph, the other is proper to people in consternation or disorder of mind.

Theseus, after the funeral of his father, paid his vows to Apollo the seventh day of Pyanepsion; for on that day the youth that returned with him safe from Crete made their entry into the city. They say, also, that the custom of boiling pulse at this feast is derived from hence; because the young men that escaped put all that was left of their provision together, and, boiling it in one common pot, feasted themselves with it, and ate it all up together. Hence, also, they carry in procession an olive branch bound about with wool (such as they then made use of in their supplications), which they call Eiresione, crowned with all sorts of fruits, to signify that scarcity and barrenness was ceased, singing in their procession this song:

> *Eiresione bring figs, and Eiresione bring loaves;*
> *Bring us honey in pints, and oil to rub on our bodies,*
> *And a strong flagon of wine, for all to go mellow to bed on.*

Although some hold opinion that this ceremony is retained in memory of the Heraclidae, who were thus entertained and brought up by the Athenians. But most are of the opinion which we have given above.

The ship wherein Theseus and the youth of Athens returned had thirty oars, and was preserved by the Athenians down even to the time of Demetrius Phalereus, for they took away the old planks as they decayed, putting in new and stronger timber in their place, insomuch that this ship became a standing example among the philosophers, for the logical question as to things that grow; one side holding that the ship remained the same, and the other contending that it was not the same.

The feast called Oschophoria, or the feast of boughs, which to this day the Athenians celebrate, was then first instituted by Theseus. For he took not with him the full number of virgins which by lot were to be carried away, but selected two youths of his acquaintance, of fair and womanish faces, but of a manly and forward spirit, and having, by frequent baths, and avoiding the heat and scorching of the sun, with a constant use of all the ointments and washes and dresses that serve to the adorning of the head or smoothing the skin or improving the complexion, in a manner changed them from what they were before, and having taught them farther to counterfeit the very voice and carriage and gait of virgins, so that there could not be the least difference perceived; he, undiscovered by any, put them into the number of the Athenian maids designed for Crete. At his return, he and these two youths led up a solemn procession, in the same habit that is now worn by those who carry the vine-branches. These branches they carry in honor of Bacchus and Ariadne, for the sake of their story before related; or rather because they happened to return in autumn, the time of gathering the grapes. The women whom they call Deipnopheræ, or supper-carriers, are taken into these ceremonies, and assist at the sacrifice, in remembrance and imitation of the mothers of the young men and virgins upon whom the lot fell, for thus they ran about bringing bread and meat to their children; and because the women then told their sons and daughters many tales and stories, to comfort and encourage them under the danger they were going upon, it has still continued a custom that at this feast old fables and tales should be told. For these particularities we are indebted to the history of Demon. There was then a place chosen out, and a temple erected in it to Theseus, and those families out of whom the tribute of the youth was gathered were appointed to pay a tax to the temple for sacrifices to him. And the house of the Phytalidae had the overseeing of these sacrifices, Theseus doing them that honor in recompense of their former hospitality.

Now, after the death of his father Aegeus, forming in his mind a great and wonderful design, he gathered together all the inhabitants of Attica into one town, and made them one people of one city, whereas before they lived dispersed, and were not easy to assemble upon any affair for the common interest. Nay, differences and even wars often occurred between them, which he by his persuasions appeased, going from township to township, and from tribe to tribe. And those of a more private and mean condition readily embracing such good advice, to those of greater power he promised a commonwealth without monarchy, a democracy, or people's government in which he should only be continued as their commander in war and the protector of their laws, all things else being equally distributed among them; and by this means brought a part of them over to his proposal. The rest, fearing his power, which was already grown very formidable, and knowing his courage and resolution, chose rather to be persuaded than forced into a compliance. He then dissolved all the distinct state-houses, council halls, and magistracies, and built one common state-house and council hall on the site of the present upper town, and gave the name of Athens to the whole state, ordaining a common feast and sacrifice, which he called Panathenaea, or the sacrifice of all the united Athenians. He instituted also another sacrifice, called Metoecia, or Feast of Migration, which is yet celebrated on the sixteenth day of Hecatombaeon. Then, as he had promised, he laid down his regal power and proceeded to order a commonwealth, entering upon this great work not without advice from the gods. For having sent to consult the oracle of Delphi concerning the fortune of his new government and city, he received this answer:

> *Son of the Pitthean maid,*
> *To your town the terms and fates,*
> *My father gives of many states.*
> *Be not anxious nor afraid;*
> *The bladder will not fail so swim*

On the waves that compass him.

Which oracle, they say, one of the sibyls long after did in a manner repeat to the Athenians, in this verse,

The bladder may be dipt, but not be drowned.

Farther yet designing to enlarge his city, he invited all strangers to come and enjoy equal privileges with the natives, and it is said that the common form, *Come hither, all ye people,* was the words that Theseus proclaimed when he thus set up a commonwealth, in a manner, for all nations. Yet he did not suffer his state, by the promiscuous multitude that flowed in, to be turned into confusion and be left without any order or degree, but was the first that divided the Commonwealth into three distinct ranks, the noblemen, the husbandmen, and artificers. To the nobility he committed the care of religion, the choice of magistrates, the teaching and dispensing of the laws, and interpretation and direction in all sacred matters; the whole city being, as it were, reduced to an exact equality, the nobles excelling the rest in honor, the husbandmen in profit, and the artificers in number. And that Theseus was the first, who, as Aristotle says, out of an inclination to popular government, parted with the regal power, Homer also seems to testify, in his catalogue of the ships, where he gives the name of *People* to the Athenians only.

He also coined money, and stamped it with the image of an ox, either in memory of the Marathonian bull, or of Taurus, whom he vanquished, or else to put his people in mind to follow husbandry; and from this coin came the expression so frequent among the Greeks, of a thing being worth ten or a hundred oxen. After this he joined Megara to Attica, and erected that famous pillar on the Isthmus, which bears an inscription of two lines, showing the bounds of the two countries that meet there. On the east side the inscription is,--

Peloponnesus there, Ionia here,

and on the west side,--

Peloponnesus here, Ionia there.

He also instituted the games, in emulation of Hercules, being ambitious that as the Greeks, by that hero's appointment, celebrated the Olympian games to the honor of Jupiter, so, by his institution, they should celebrate the Isthmian to the honor of Neptune. For those that were there before observed, dedicated to Melicerta, were performed privately in the night, and had the form rather of a religious rite than of an open spectacle or public feast. There are some who say that the Isthmian games were first instituted in memory of Sciron, Theseus thus making expiation for his death, upon account of the nearness of kindred between them, Sciron being the son of Canethus and Heniocha, the daughter of Pittheus; though others write that Sinnis, not Sciron, was their son, and that to his honor, and not to the other's, these games were ordained by Theseus. At the same time he made an agreement with the Corinthians, that they should allow those that came from Athens to the celebration of the Isthmian games as much space of honor before the rest to behold the spectacle in, as the sail of the ship that brought them thither, stretched to its full extent, could cover; so Hellanicus and Andro of Halicarnassus have established.

Concerning his voyage into the Euxine Sea, Philochorus and some others write that he made it with Hercules, offering him his service in the war against the Amazons, and had Antiope given him for the reward of his valor; but the greater number, of whom are Pherecydes, Hellanicus, and w:Herodorus, write that he made this voyage many years after Hercules, with a navy under his own command, and took the Amazon prisoner, the more probable story, for we do not read that any other, of all those that accompanied him in this action, took any Amazon prisoner. w:Bion adds, that, to take her, he had to use deceit and fly away; for the Amazons, he says, being naturally lovers of men, were so far from avoiding Theseus when he touched upon their coasts, that they sent him presents to his ship; but he, having invited Antiope, who brought them, to come aboard, immediately set sail and carried her away. An author named Menecrates, that wrote the History of Nicaea in Bithynia, adds, that Theseus, having Antiope aboard his vessel, cruised for some time about those coasts, and that there were in the same ship three young men of Athens, that accompanied him in this voyage, all brothers, whose names were Euneos, Thoas, and Soloon. The last of these fell desperately in love with Antiope; and, escaping the notice of the rest, revealed the secret only to one of his most intimate acquaintance, and employed him to disclose his passion to Antiope, she rejected his pretenses with a very positive denial, yet treated the matter with much gentleness and discretion, and made no complaint to Theseus of any thing that had happened; but Soloon, the thing being desperate, leaped into a river near the seaside and drowned himself. As soon as Theseus was acquainted with his death, and his unhappy love that was the cause of it, he was extremely distressed, and, in the height of his grief, an oracle which he had formerly received at Delphi came into his mind, for he had been commanded by the priestess of Apollo Pythius, that, wherever in a strange land he was most sorrowful and under the greatest affliction, he should build a city there, and leave some of his followers to be governors of the place. For this cause he there founded a city, which he called, from the name of Apollo, Pythopolis, and, in honor of the unfortunate youth, he named the river that runs by it Soloon, and left the two surviving brothers entrusted with the care of the government and laws, joining with them Hermus, one of the nobility of Athens, from whom a place in the city is called the House of Hermus; though by an error in the accent it has been taken for the House of Hermes, or Mercury, and the honor that was designed to the hero transferred to the god.

This was the origin and cause of the Amazonian invasion of Attica, which would seem to have been no slight or womanish enterprise. For it is impossible that they should have placed their camp in the very city, and joined battle close by the Pnyx and the hill called Museum, unless, having first conquered the country round about, they had thus with impunity advanced to the city. That they made so long a journey by land, and passed the Cimmerian Bosphorus when frozen, as Hellanicus writes, is difficult to be believed. That they encamped all but in the city is certain, and may be sufficiently confirmed by the names that the places thereabout yet retain, and the graves and monuments of those that fell in the battle. Both armies being in sight, there was a long pause and doubt on each side which should give the first onset; at last Theseus, having sacrificed to Fear, in obedience to the command of an oracle he had received, gave them battle; and this happened in the month of Boedromion, in which to this very day the Athenians celebrate the Feast Boedromia. Clidemus, desirous to be very circumstantial, writes that the left wing of the Amazons moved towards the place which is yet called Amazonium and the right towards the Pnyx, near Chrysa, that with this wing the Athenians, issuing from behind the Museum, engaged, and that the graves of those that were slain are to be seen in the street that leads to the gate called the Piraic, by the chapel of the hero Chalcodon; and that here the Athenians were routed, and gave way before the women, as far as to the temple of the Furies, but, fresh supplies coming in from the Palladium, Ardettus, and the Lyceum, they charged their right wing, and beat them back into their tents, in which action a great number of the Amazons were slain. At length, after four months, a peace was concluded between them by the mediation of Hippolyta (for so this historian calls the Amazon whom Theseus married, and not Antiope), though others write that she was slain with a dart by Molpadia, while fighting by Theseus's side, and that the pillar which stands by the temple of Olympian Earth was erected to her honor. Nor is it to be wondered at, that in events of such antiquity, history should be in disorder. For indeed we are also told that those of the Amazons that were wounded were privately sent away by Antiope to Chalcis, where many by her care recovered, but some that died were buried there in the place that is to this time called Amazonium. That this war, however, was ended by a treaty is evident, both from the name of the place adjoining to the temple of Theseus, called, from the solemn oath there taken, Horcomosium; and also from the ancient sacrifice which used to be celebrated to the Amazons the day before the Feast of Theseus. The Megarians also show a spot in their city where some Amazons were buried, on the way from the market to a place called Rhus, where the building in the shape of a lozenge stands. It is said, likewise, that others of them were slain near Charonea, and buried near the little rivulet, formerly called Thermodon, but now Haemon, of which an account is given in the life of Demosthenes. It appears further that the passage of the Amazons through Thessaly was not without opposition, for there are yet shown many tombs of them near w:Scotussa and Cynoscephalae.

This is as much as is worth telling concerning the Amazons. For the account which the author of the poem called the *Theseid* gives of this rising of the Amazons, how Antiope, to revenge herself upon Theseus for refusing her and marrying Phaedra, came down upon the city with her train of Amazons, whom Hercules slew, is manifestly nothing else but fable and invention. It is true, indeed, that Theseus married Phaedra, but that was after the death of Antiope, by whom he had a son called Hippolytus, or, as Pindar writes, Demophon. The calamities which befell Phaedra and this son, since none of the historians have contradicted the tragic poets that have written of them, we must suppose happened as represented uniformly by them.

There are also other traditions of the marriages of Theseus, neither honorable in their occasions nor fortunate in their events, which yet were never represented in the Greek plays. For he is said to have carried off Anaxo, a Troezenian, and, having slain Sinnis and Cercyon, to have ravished their daughters; to have married Peribœa, the mother of Ajax, and then Pherebœa, and then Iope, the daughter of Iphicles. And further, he is accused of deserting Ariadne (as is before related), being in love with Ægle the daughter of Panopeus, neither justly nor honorably; and lastly, of the rape of Helen, which filled all Attica with war and blood, and was in the end the occasion of his banishment and death, as will presently be related.

Herodorus is of opinion, that though there were many famous expeditions undertaken by the bravest men of his time, yet Theseus never joined in any of them, once only excepted, with the Lapithae, in their war against the Centaurs; but others say that he accompanied Jason to Colchis and Meleager to the slaying of the Calydonian boar, and that hence it came to be a proverb, *Not without Theseus;* that he himself, however, without aid of any one, performed many glorious exploits, and that from him began the saying, *He is a second Hercules.* He also joined Adrastus in recovering the bodies of those that were slain before Thebes, but not as Euripides in his tragedy says, by force of arms, but by persuasion and mutual agreement and composition, for so the greater part of the historians write; Philochorus adds further that this was the first treaty that ever was made for the recovering the bodies of the dead, but in the history of Hercules it is shown that it was he who first gave leave to his enemies to carry off their slain. The burying-places of the most part are yet to be seen in the village called Eleutherae; those of the commanders, at Eleusis, where Theseus allotted them a place, to oblige Adrastus. The story of Euripides in his Suppliants is disproved by Aeschylus in his Eleusinians, where Theseus himself relates the facts as here told.

The celebrated friendship between Theseus and Pirithoüs is said to have been thus begun: the fame of the strength and valor of Theseus being spread through Greece, Pirithoüs was desirous to make a trial and proof of it himself, and to this end seized a herd of oxen which belonged to Theseus, and was driving them away from Marathon, and, when news was brought that Theseus pursued him in arms, he did not fly, but turned back and went to meet him. But as soon as they had viewed one another, each so admired the gracefulness and beauty, and was seized with such a respect for the courage, of the other, that they forgot all thoughts of fighting; and Pirithoüs, first stretching out his hand to Theseus, bade him be judge in this case himself, and promised to submit willingly to any penalty he should impose. But Theseus not only forgave him all, but entreated him to be his friend and brother in arms; and they ratified their friendship by oaths. After this Pirithoüs married Deidamia, and invited Theseus to the wedding, entreating him to come and see his country, and make acquaintance with the Lapithae; he had at the same time invited the Centaurs to the feast, who growing hot with wine and beginning to be insolent and wild, and offering violence to the women, the Lapithae took immediate revenge upon them, slaying many of them upon the place, and afterwards, having overcome them in battle, drove the whole race of them out of their country, Theseus all along taking their part and fighting on their side. But Herodorus gives a different relation of these things: that Theseus came not to the assistance of the Lapithae till the war was already begun; and that it was in this journey that he had the first sight of Hercules, having made it his business to find him out at Trachis, where he had chosen to rest himself after all his wanderings and his labors; and that this interview was honorably performed on each part, with extreme respect, good-will, and admiration of each other. Yet it is more credible, as others write, that there were, before, frequent interviews between them, and that it was by the means of Theseus that Hercules was initiated at Eleusis, and purified before initiation, upon account of several rash actions of his former life.

Theseus was now fifty years old, as Hellanicus states, when he carried off Helen, who was yet too young to be married. Some writers, to take away this accusation of one of the greatest crimes laid to his charge, say, that he did not steal away Helen himself, but that Idas and Lynceus were the ravishers, who brought her to him, and committed her to his charge, and that, therefore, he refused to restore her at the demand of Castor and Pollux; or, indeed, they say her own father, Tyndarus, had sent her to be kept by him, for fear of Enarophorus, the son of Hippocoon, who would have carried her away by force when she was yet a child. But the most probable account, and that which has most witnesses on its side, is this: Theseus and Pirithoüs went both together to Sparta, and, having seized the young lady as she was dancing in the temple of Diana Orthia, fled away with her. There were presently men in arms sent to pursue, but they followed no further than to Tegea; and Theseus and Pirithoüs, being now out of danger, having passed through Peloponnesus, made an agreement between themselves, that he to whom the lot should fall should have Helen to his wife, but should be obliged to assist in procuring another for his friend. The lot fell upon Theseus, who conveyed her to Aphidnae, not being yet marriageable, and delivered her to one of his allies, called Aphidnus, and, having sent his mother Aethra after to take care of her, desired him to keep them so secretly, that none might know where they were; which done, to return the same service to his friend Pirithoüs, he accompanied him in his journey to Epirus, in order to steal away the king of the Molossians' daughter. The king, his own name being w:Aidoneus, or Pluto, called his wife Proserpina, and his daughter

Cora, and a great dog which he kept Cerberus, with whom he ordered all that came as suitors to his daughter to fight, and promised her to him that should overcome the beast. But having been informed that the design of Pirithoüs and his companion was not to court his daughter, but to force her away, he caused them both to be seized, and threw Pirithoüs to be torn in pieces by his dog, and put Theseus into prison, and kept him.

About this time, Menestheus, the son of Peteus, grandson of Orneus, and great-grandson to Erechtheus, the first man that is recorded to have affected popularity and ingratiated himself with the multitude, stirred up and exasperated the most eminent men of the city, who had long borne a secret grudge to Theseus, conceiving that he had robbed them of their several little kingdoms and lordships, and, having pent them all up in one city, was using them as his subjects and slaves. He put also the meaner people into commotion, telling them, that, deluded with a mere dream of liberty, though indeed they were deprived both of that and of their proper homes and religious usages, instead of many good and gracious kings of their own, they had given themselves up to be lorded over by a new-comer and a stranger. Whilst he was thus busied in infecting the minds of the citizens, the war that Castor and Pollux brought against Athens came very opportunely to further the sedition he had been promoting, and some say that he by his persuasions was wholly the cause of their invading the city. At their first approach, they committed no acts of hostility, but peaceably demanded their sister Helen; but the Athenians returning answer that they neither had her there nor knew where she was disposed of, they prepared to assault the city, when Academus, having, by whatever means, found it out, disclosed to them that she was secretly kept at Aphidnae. For which reason he was both highly honored during his life by Castor and Pollux, and the Lacedaemonians, when often in aftertimes they made incursions into Attica, and destroyed all the country round about, spared the Academy for the sake of Academus. But Dicaearchus writes that there were two Arcadians in the army of Castor and Pollux, the one called Echedemus and the other w:Marathus; from the first that which is now called Academia was then named Echedemia, and the village Marathon had its name from the other, who, to fulfill some oracle, voluntarily offered himself to be made a sacrifice before battle. As soon as they were arrived at Aphidnae, they overcame their enemies in a set battle, and then assaulted and took the town. And here, they say, Alycus, the son of Sciron, was slain, of the party of the Dioscuri (Castor and Pollux), from whom a place in Megara, where he was buried, is called Alycus to this day. And Hereas writes that it was Theseus himself that killed him, in witness of which he cites these verses concerning Alycus

> *And Alycus, upon Aphidna's plain*
> *By Theseus in the cause of Helen slain.*

Though it is not at all probable that Theseus himself was there when both the city and his mother were taken.

Aphidnae being won by Castor and Pollux, and the city of Athens being in consternation, Menestheus persuaded the people to open their gates, and receive them with all manner of friendship, for they were, he told them, at enmity with none but Theseus, who had first injured them, and were benefactors and saviors to all mankind beside. And their behavior gave credit to those promises; for, having made themselves absolute masters of the place, they demanded no more than to be initiated, since they were as nearly related to the city as Hercules was, who had received the same honor. This their desire they easily obtained, and were adopted by Aphidnus, as Hercules had been by Pylius. They were honored also like gods, and were called by a new name, Anaces, either from the *cessation* (Anokhe) of the war, or from the *care* they took that none should suffer any injury, though there was so great an army within the walls; for the phrase *anăkōs ĕkhein* is used of those who look to or care for any thing; kings for this reason, perhaps, are called *anactes*. Others say, that from the appearance of their star in the heavens, they were thus called, for in the Attic dialect this name comes very near the words that signify *above*.

Some say that Aethra, Theseus's mother, was here taken prisoner, and carried to Lacedaemon, and from thence went away with Helen to Troy, alleging this verse of Homer, to prove that she waited upon Helen,

Aethra of Pittheus born, and large-eyed Clymene.

Others reject this verse as none of Homer's, as they do likewise the whole fable of Munychus, who, the story says, was the son of Demophon and Laodice, born secretly, and brought up by Aethra at Troy. But Ister, in the thirteenth book of his Attic History, gives us an account of Aethra, different yet from all the rest: that Achilles and Patroclus overcame Paris in Thessaly, near the river w:Sperchius, but that Hector took and plundered the city of the Troezenians, and made Aethra prisoner there. But this seems a groundless tale.

Now Hercules, passing by the Molossians, was entertained in his way by Aidoneus the king, who, in conversation, accidentally spoke of the journey of Theseus and Pirithoüs into his country, of what they had designed to do, and what they were forced to suffer. Hercules was much grieved for the inglorious death of the one and the miserable condition of the other. As for Pirithoüs, he thought it useless to complain; but begged to have Theseus released for his sake, and obtained that favor from the king.

Theseus, being thus set at liberty, returned to Athens, where his friends were not yet wholly suppressed, and dedicated to Hercules all the sacred places which the city had set apart for himself, changing their names from Thesea to Heraclea, four only excepted, as Philochorus writes. And wishing immediately to resume the first place in the commonwealth, and manage the state as before, he soon found himself involved in factions and troubles; those who long had hated him had now added to their hatred contempt; and the minds of the people were so generally corrupted, that, instead of obeying commands with silence, they expected to be flattered into their duty. He had some thoughts to have reduced them by force, but was overpowered by demagogues and factions. And at last, despairing of any good success of his affairs in Athens, he sent away his children privately to Euboea, commending them to the care of Elephenor, the son of Chalcodon; and he himself, having solemnly cursed the people of Athens in the village of Gargettus, in which there yet remains the place called Araterion, or the place of cursing, sailed to Scyros, where he had lands left him by his father, and friendship, as he thought, with those of the island.

Lycomedes was then king of Scyros. Theseus, therefore, addressed himself to him, and desired to have his lands put into his possession, as designing to settle and to dwell there, though others say that he came to beg his assistance against the Athenians. But Lycomedes, either jealous of the glory of so great a man, or to gratify Menestheus, having led him up to the highest cliff of the island, on pretense of showing him from thence the lands that he desired, threw him headlong down from the rock, and killed him. Others say he fell down of himself by a slip of his foot, as he was walking there, according to his custom, after supper. At that time there was no notice taken, nor were any concerned for his death, but Menestheus quietly possessed the kingdom of Athens. His sons were brought up in a private condition, and accompanied Elephenor to the Trojan war, but, after the decease of Menestheus in that expedition, returned to Athens, and recovered the government.

But in succeeding ages, beside several other circumstances that moved the Athenians to honor Theseus as a demigod, in the battle which was fought at Marathon against the Medes, many of the soldiers believed they saw an apparition of Theseus in arms, rushing on at the head of them against the barbarians. And after the Median war, Phaedo being archon of Athens, the Athenians, consulting the oracle at Delphi, were commanded to gather together the bones of Theseus, and, laying them in some honorable place, keep them as sacred in the city. But it was very difficult to recover these relics, or so much as to find out the place where they lay, on account of the inhospitable and savage temper of the barbarous people that inhabited the island. Nevertheless, afterwards, when Cimon took the island (as is related in his life), and had a great ambition to find out the place where Theseus was buried, he, by chance, spied an eagle upon a rising ground pecking with her beak and tearing up the earth with her talons, when on the sudden it came into his mind, as it were by some divine inspiration, to dig there, and search for the bones of Theseus. There were found in that place a coffin of a man of more than ordinary size, and a brazen spear-head, and a sword lying by it, all which he took aboard his galley and brought with him to Athens. Upon which the Athenians, greatly delighted, went out to meet and receive the relics with splendid processions and with sacrifices, as if it were Theseus himself returning alive to the city.

He lies interred in the middle of the city, near the present gymnasium. His tomb is a sanctuary and refuge for slaves, and all those of mean condition that fly from the persecution of men in power, in memory that Theseus while he lived was an assister and protector of the distressed, and never refused the petitions of the afflicted that fled to him. The chief and most solemn sacrifice which they celebrate to him is kept on the eighth day of Pyanepsion, on which he returned with the Athenian young men from Crete. Besides which, they sacrifice to him on the eighth day of every month, either because he returned from Troezen the eighth day of Hecatombaeon, as Diodorus the geographer writes, or else thinking that number to be proper to him, because he was reputed to be born of Neptune, because they sacrifice to Neptune on the eighth day of every month. The number eight being the first cube of an even number, and the double of the first square, seemed to be an emblem of the steadfast and immovable power of this god, who from thence has the names of Asphalius and Gaeiochus, that is, the establisher and stayer of the earth.

Printed in Great Britain
by Amazon